Road Called

Chaos

Taking the
FIRST STEPS
Toward
Organization

Audrey Thomas

Expert Publishing, Inc.
Andover, Minnesota

ISBN 1-931945-23-3

Library of Congress Catalog Number: 2004109443

Printed in the United States of America

First Printing: August 2004

07 06 05 04   6 5 4 3 2 1

Expert Publishing, Inc.
14314 Thrush Street NW
Andover, MN 55304-3330
1-877-755-4966
www.expertpublishinginc.com

To Tone

My encourager, my partner, my best friend.

Long ago we discussed the importance of living in an environment that fostered peace and contentment within our family. That conversation has been my motivation to continually strive to bring peace and order to our busy lives.

Without you, I would have never attempted this book. And I'd probably be living in chaos.

*"It is best to do things systematically,
since we are only human, and disorder
is our worst enemy."*

—Hesiod

"What Hesiod said."
—Organized Audrey

Table of

Contents

Chapter 1

Why Get Organized?

You're late for a meeting, there's no washer fluid in the car, your pantyhose have a run in them, and the cat hoarked up a hairball in your shoe. Not exactly the picture of stress-free living, is it?

Chaos, in a word, stinks.

It's no surprise: Disorder breeds stress. It throws our world—and the worlds of our family and coworkers—into disarray. It fosters feelings of failure, defeat, and even disgust that can linger for decades. Being disorganized, whether at home or at work, affects a person's "emotional bottom line." It impacts our relationships with other people. If left unchecked, it can eat away at our sense of well-being, until there's nothing left but a frazzled, frenzied shadow of our former selves. It makes us feel as if our lives have spun out of control.

Disorganization doesn't show up in medical texts, and its treatment isn't covered by insurance companies. But it might as well be; it's an epidemic. Believe it or not, there's even a National Study Group for the Chronically Disorganized (www.nsgcd.org) out there, researching exactly what makes our organizational—and disorganizational—urges tick. Makes you think of a lab full of white-coated scientists bustling among beakers and high-tech gizmos, searching for a cure for this debilitating disease, right? Well, it's not quite that clinical. But they are asking some intriguing questions about why our lives are so chaotic.

Good thing, too. Like many actual diseases, disorganization can make you feel physically and emotionally ill, cause rifts in families, and plunge a person into a downward spiral they have a hard time reversing. You might be surprised at just how much being disorganized affects us, both as individuals and as a society.

Statistics say an average person spends 150 hours a year looking for lost information. One hundred and fifty hours! That's nearly four work weeks wasted trying to find a misplaced phone number, mislaid tool, or mislabeled file. And I don't know about you, but when I've misplaced something, it frustrates me to no end as I turn the place upside down looking for it. The longer I look, the grumpier I get.

And it's not just at home. When a coworker struggling with disorganization loses a document or forgets about a meeting, it impacts a lot of people—and the company's bottom line. Think of all the millions of dollars a year frittered away on missed appointments, lost invoices, or unstructured meetings.

■ FEELING LOST?

Order, on the other hand, is healthy. We all know what it's like when everything's running smoothly: Your shoes are clean, your shirt is pressed, the car has a full tank of gas, the kids are all ready for school. Ain't life grand!

When my kids reached the toddler stage, something pretty basic, but very important, occurred to me: Children thrive when they have order in their lives. They flourish when they have a sense of calm to their surroundings. They succeed when they know that their lives won't constantly be full of drama. They appreciate stability.

And, you know what? So do I.

Possibly the greatest benefit of getting organized is that order cuts down on stress. Without sounding too pie-in-the-sky, I've found that there's one undeniable truth when it comes to organization: order fosters peace and harmony.

People who've taken the first steps toward getting organized—me included—find we reap several benefits by embracing order. We'll cover these more in-depth throughout the book, but here's a quick look at some of the benefits of finding the way off the Road Called Chaos.

Order fosters peace and harmony.

Save time. With the right systems in place, we don't waste minutes, hours, or days looking for things. Who couldn't find a better use for time spent trying to track down a misplaced phone number, an email address, or the car keys?

Save money. Eliminating chaos from our lives makes it easier to keep an eye on our belongings. When we're organized, stuff doesn't get lost as easily. We don't have to purchase a replacement item, only to eventually discover the "lost" flashlight, birthday gift, or can of peas in the back of the cupboard.

Get rid of guilt and shame. Feeling bad about being disorganized can really sap a lot of emotional energy. Getting our life in order helps banish those counterproductive feelings.

Protect ourselves. I've seen people use another person's disorganization to control them. When you're disorganized, being taken advantage of is a real possibility. A coworker could tell you, "Why, you must have lost that document I gave you," and you assume it's true. A family member could wreak havoc on your finances, or squirrel money away, and you'd have no idea.

Avoid passing on disorganized habits to our children. It's amazing how many people who wrestle with disorganization grew up in a chaotic household where they lacked opportunities to learn organizational skills. Embracing order helps us break that chain with our own kids.

■ MAKING A CHANGE

Sometimes we're well aware that we need to change the way we live. We know it. Others know it. Other times, we may have come to rely on a disorganized routine so much that we've actually forgotten what it's like to experience tranquility. When we first start discussing their disorganization, many clients tell me, "I've lived this way most of my life; it's probably easier just to continue—even though I'm miserable."

My friend Sara thrives on chaos. Or, at least she used to think so. She learned early on to function in panic mode, and that's where she's stayed. Her kids rarely have matching socks. They eat fast food all the time; she's not able to plan ahead enough to coordinate sit-down meals.

Up until recently, Sara claimed she liked living like this. But she's starting to see how her disorganization affects the other people in her life. During one particularly stressful day of zipping around from errand to appointment, her young son came up to her, put his head on her lap and said, "Mommy, I feel like I'm in a race all the time." Leave it to a young child to help her see the light. That encounter gave her pause, and helped her become aware of the environment she was creating for her loved ones. She'd forgotten what it was like to live in an organized world.

■ SIMPLE ADVICE, IMPORTANT LESSONS

With this book, my goal is to pass along the lessons I've learned during my years as an organizing consultant and speaker. I'll also share some of the paths my clients have taken on the journey toward order. It's designed to lay the groundwork to help you embark on a whole new way of living. I've changed the names and some identifying details, but every story you're about to read is true.

Much of what follows may seem like simple advice, and, in a way, it is. But it's important information, chopped into bite-sized pieces. If you're like most of the people I work with, the last thing you need is another thick book sitting by the side of your bed, mocking you with huge chapters of information you'll never find enough time to wade through. So this book is designed to be quickly digested on a plane, while you're waiting for a meeting, or when you get a break after dropping the kids off at soccer practice.

I hope that by reading these tips, techniques, and case studies you'll discover that taking the first steps on the road to organization is an achievable goal. And you're even more likely to turn your willingness to change into a long-term organizational lifestyle if you take a good look at your personality type and learning style before you begin. From there, you'll work on building an organizational program based on your own unique situation. No cookie-cutter approach here. This is all about you.

Organization is really about creating a more peaceful environment for you, your family, and your coworkers. Disorganization breeds chaos. And if you're anything like the people I work with, you've got too much chaos in your life as it is.

Chapter 2

Road Blocks Contributing to Disorganization

Feel like you're drowning in disorganization? You're not the only one. Millions of people struggle with many of the same challenges you're likely facing. In fact, I'd go so far as to suggest that every one of us, no matter how organized we look on the surface, could use a refresher course in banishing chaos from our lives.

A librarian friend once told me that the books her library had to replace most often were—surprise—books on how to get organized. Patrons with a desire to embrace order would check them out and take them home, but because they lacked organizational skills, they'd eventually lose the books in a pile of clutter.

There's no shortage of reasons people realize they need help in the organization department. Like my friend Sara, maybe the message comes from an innocent family member caught in the disorganizational tornado. Maybe an employer gives an ultimatum. ("You've lost one too many files. Get help or you're fired.") Maybe the ultimatum comes from a spouse or significant other. ("I can't live like this anymore. Get help or I'm leaving.") Or maybe it simply dawns on them, "There's got to be a better way to live."

Before we move forward, it's important to take a look at where we've been. The reasons behind disorganization are as countless and varied as the personalities of the people chaos affects. See how many of these may apply to your situation.

Too many interests. Sometimes people are so busy they fail to leave time in their schedules to deal with everyday things like paying bills, sorting the mail, or getting an oil change. Simply having too many appointments, events, and activities on the calendar results in an inability to stay focused.

Distraction. Whether it's the increased interruptions that come with raising children or dealing with Attention Deficit Disorder (ADD) or similar tendencies, distractions often conspire to cause lives to spin out of control.

Procrastination. Putting off decisions and chores creates lots of unfinished business, and only results in putting more "to-dos" on tomorrow's list. Here's a critical thing to remember: clutter is a result of delayed decisions. You'll hear me mention it again and again, but this is truly one of the most important realizations on the road to getting organized.

Perfectionism. Some people won't start a job or organizational regimen until they believe they'll be able to do it perfectly. Postponing taking the first steps toward organization can lead to taking no steps at all. Or sometimes it's a partner's perfectionism

Clutter is a result of delayed decisions.

that causes trouble. Several people have confided in me that they *want* to get organized, but they fear they won't meet their spouse's high organizational standards.

Feelings of being overwhelmed. We're creatures of habit, and some people are too frightened to try to get organized. They think, "It's so much easier just to live a cluttered life and keep living as I've always lived."

Getting organized can be a big job, and can be intimidating to some people. I asked one client to list three places in her house she needed help getting organized. "Upstairs, downstairs, and the basement," she sighed, exasperated. Not knowing where or how to begin only exacerbates an "it's too big of an undertaking" mentality and can sabotage your efforts before they even begin.

Rebelliousness. When we start discussing their family background, some clients tell me that when they were kids, their mother ruled the household like a military barracks, forcing them to keep their rooms ship-shape all the time. So now that they're adults, they're rebelling by throwing their clothes wherever they please. While this form of acting out beats taking drugs or overthrowing a small country, it can result in a disorganized lifestyle.

Role models. We learn to do things from our parents, both consciously and subconsciously. We buy the same brands as Mom did. We find ourselves using the same vocal inflections when we tell our kids to clean their rooms. Without placing blame, it's important to realize our parents played a big role in how we live today. One of my clients told me she realized that her mother taught her every intricacy about homemaking skills, but not a single thing about filing. A lack of organizational groundwork during childhood can become a big factor in allowing chaos to direct our adult lives.

Sentimentality. Some folks keep just about everything, storing each school paper, macaroni sculpture, or baby's crib for years and years. When we focus on keeping the material thing—rather than the memory behind it— our closets and spare rooms pay the price.

Major life changes. Big events, from having children to receiving a promotion to caring for an aging parent, all play a role in our ability to maintain an organized lifestyle. Over the years, I've discovered that many people can point to a major life change as the time when their disorganization began. Marriage, birth, death of a loved one, illness or diagnosis, a new job—the list goes on and on. And these events have a huge impact on our capacity to stay organized. When I discuss this issue with my clients they often remark, "Wow, I've really been busy with a lot! It's no wonder I've fallen behind." It helps to know that you don't have to be a "super human" while balancing everything that's competing for your attention. In other words, don't get hung up on the guilt you have regarding disorganization. It's simply time to free yourself from the past and move forward.

Illness and death can deal a particularly harsh blow to a person's ability to stay afloat. I know that when my own mother had a stroke, I was late with my mortgage payment for the first time in seventeen years. One of my clients found herself in a similar position, and all she could do was watch helplessly as her life spun out of control.

■ ■ ■ Case Study: Alice ■ ■ ■

Alice was always organized, managing a job, a household, and three children. Then her husband, Tom, was diagnosed with cancer, and everything began to change. During Tom's illness, Alice took a leave of absence from her job to take care of her husband, and she quickly realized she had stepped onto a roller coaster. She was able to maintain the mounting pile of insurance and health records, but everything else went by the wayside. Tom eventually succumbed to cancer, and after his death, Alice found herself alone, and in surroundings that had grown out of control during her husband's illness.

After nearly a year of existing in a quagmire of chaos, she confided in her grown children that she was looking for help to get back on track. So, for Mother's Day, they bought her a gift certificate for my organizing services. Alice cried when she received it. She was ready.

Alice's story is a classic case of what happens when a life-changing event occurs in a person's life. By the time she realized chaos had overtaken her existence, she was too overwhelmed to know where to start.

When we first met, she told me it was her number one priority to get the family room back into shape. During Tom's illness, the grandchildren had to put on hold their beloved play dates and overnight visits to Grandma and Grandpa's house. She wanted to create a space just for them—complete with books, toys, puzzles, and crafts.

In the months after Tom's passing, Alice had tackled a much-needed kitchen remodeling project. Consequently, many of the kitchen's possessions had been boxed up and temporarily placed in the family room. In fact, the family room resembled a storage unit, with crates, small appliances, and utensils stacked from wall to wall.

So, we took a step backwards and analyzed where to begin. In order to transform the family room into "The Grandkids' Room," we had to first focus our attention on the kitchen.

Giving to others is always a win-win for everyone involved

While working together, Alice shared sweet memories with me of life with Tom. Alice was blessed with a mother's heart, nurturing and putting others' needs before her own. One of the ways she had provided for her family in the past was to cook delicious, large meals. After Tom's passing her youngest child headed off to college and Alice was now not only a widow, but an empty-nester as well. But Alice had continued grocery shopping as if the house was still buzzing with activity. I made the suggestion to donate much of her excess food to her favorite food shelf. She was thrilled with this idea; Alice gained needed cupboard space and at the same time received much joy providing food for the needy. Giving to others is always a win-win for everyone involved.

The whole process worked because we set a plan into motion by determining the best place to begin, and we moved forward from there. And along the way, Alice was able to not only allow herself to recover from the memories of her husband's illness, but she was able to help other people as well. As we progressed through the organizing sessions, Alice commented about how life changing the whole experience had been for her. She called it therapy, and, in a way, it was.

She has since found it possible to jump back into life, and she's enjoying her children and grandchildren with a renewed focus and enthusiasm.

∎ NEW SPACES, NEW CHALLENGES

It doesn't have to be a change as dramatic as losing a loved one. Often, moving into a new office or home can wreak havoc on our ability to organize. And unless we're wired to notice and respond to the small details that are throwing us out of whack, it can turn into trouble.

∎ ∎ ∎ CASE STUDY: MIKE ∎ ∎ ∎

Mike is a salesman who absolutely thrives on cold calling and closing the deal. But he also fits the mold of a typical left-handed person—creative and artistic. For the past several years, he had set sales records. But he recently moved into a new office in his fiancée's house, and he found that something felt *off*. He was so focused on the big picture, he wasn't paying attention to the details in his new office that were throwing a wrench into his otherwise successful way of doing business.

When he initially moved into this space, he very quickly set up his computer, printer, scanner, and fax. After he settled in, he realized the setup wasn't ideal, but he dreaded unhooking the many cords scattered across the floor, so he decided he would just "live with it" the way it was.

After meeting with Mike, I soon realized that the way he laid out his office hindered his ability to work efficiently. His equipment, supplies, and files didn't flow well. His main source of stress came from the fact that he had to keep getting out of his chair dozens of times throughout the day whenever he wanted to fax, scan, print, or put together an information package. Without realizing it, Mike had begun doing less cold calling because the things he needed to support these sales calls were not easily at hand.

The first thing we did was take everything out of the office and start from scratch. This took some convincing; after all, he didn't look forward to dismantling the heap of spaghetti cords and then reconnecting them. I wanted to make sure he felt drawn to the office, rather than repelled. The room was lit very poorly, so I suggested track lighting to brighten the place up. Since he was creative, I knew he'd respond well to having his own personal touches in the office, so we traded his significant other's frilly knick-knacks for his own favorite items. His desk was overly large for such a tiny space; we simply replaced it with a smaller one.

But the biggest change we made was relatively simple, yet it made a huge difference in his ability to work efficiently. To remove the stress of constantly getting up to use different pieces of equipment or put together information packets, we replaced the awkward printer stand with an eight-foot work table to house his printer, fax, scanner, and office supplies that had been haphazardly stored in the closet. And above the table we hung a stationery sorter to store all the materials and supplies Mike sends out to customers after speaking with them on the phone. Everything was now within arm's reach, and we eliminated the constant interruption of having to get up and sit down again and again.

You should have seen the relief come over his face when he saw the finished room. Adding the stationery sorter was the breakthrough Mike was looking for, and it allowed him to focus his energy on dealing with customers, not hunting for the right-sized envelope. Making that one simple change allowed him to clear away the clutter—both physical and mental—and concentrate on making sales once again.

■ CLEARING MENTAL CLUTTER

I've never met anyone who said they like messy rooms. I've never heard any recording artist, painter, or writer say they seek messy rooms so their creativity could flow better. In fact, it's just the opposite. When it comes to concentrating on a project or relaxing to read a book, we welcome an orderly space.

I often tell my clients that when they enter a room, their brain needs to process everything their eyes are taking in. And if the room is disorganized or chaotic, they have to process a lot more information than if the room isn't in disarray. When you enter a room with clutter poking out of every crevice, your brain starts to react to all the unrest. It might be subtle, it might barely register—on the surface, anyway—but clutter is taking up valuable hard-drive space in your mind. Physical disorder promotes mental disorder.

I know that when it comes to writing, I do a lot better when the papers on my desk are picked up, filed, and my office is orderly. This allows me to concentrate on the task at hand, and not everything surrounding me. Disorganization acts as mental interruption. It gets in the way.

Physical clutter can have an impact on the decisions we make, even how much we enjoy various aspects of our lives. If the kids open their toy box and realize their favorite plaything is buried all the way at the bottom of the heap, they may have the tendency to watch a video versus digging through the mess to find what they really want.

A cluttered schedule can also impact our ability to operate efficiently. When our calendars are jam-packed with events, practices, and meetings, we may find it difficult to focus on or truly enjoy each activity. Sometimes children are running from one event to the next, when all they really want is some low-stress playtime at home with siblings and neighbors. And all Mom and Dad want is to have dinner around the table as a family.

■ RECOGNIZING ROAD BLOCKS

Fear. Distraction. Sentimentality. Perfectionism. These are all valid reasons why individuals struggle with disorganization.

Recognizing your disorganization and identifying current roadblocks are the first steps toward putting chaos aside and starting your journey down the path toward order.

Chapter 3

Getting Ready to Hit the Road

I've had people tell me, "I was born disorganized. I don't have a choice." Or, "I don't think it's possible for me to live any other way." And while it might feel that way, it's simply not true. Just because you were born into an organizationally challenged family or have spent decades in disorder doesn't mean you can't learn how to purge some of the chaos from your life.

I want you to think back to life before computers. Okay, if you're twenty-something you may have trouble with this one. But I can recall the first time I heard about "the mouse," and learned to highlight, click, and drag. And then a few years later came the Internet and email.

Some of us found it necessary to take computer classes to learn specific word processing, spreadsheet, and presentation programs. Others were naturals and caught on quickly without much coaching or training. For me, working with a computer has become second nature. And I feel isolated from the world when my computer is out of commission.

Learning organizational skills is no different. It is a skill, not a gene you're born with. Yes, some people pick it up more quickly than others. But rest assured, it can be learned.

It's not impossible to change. In fact, I've seen many previously disorganized people learn—and embrace—organized tendencies.

■ A CHANGE IN PERSPECTIVE

It isn't uncommon for disorganized people to feel shame. Some say they feel like children because they're constantly losing things and they'd be mortified if their coworkers saw how they actually lived. Many people know they have a problem, but they don't know how to start solving it. The thing to keep in mind as you're moving forward is that perspective can change. You can adopt the necessary habits.

> *Organization is a skill, not a gene you're born with.*

It's a journey, but the goal is to train yourself with an attitude of "I *want* to clean out the closet" instead of "I guess I *need* to clean out the closet." It's a small—but critical—difference. And as we say in our house, "Attitude is everything."

Attitude is everything.

■ SLOW AND STEADY WINS THE RACE

As I've already said, organization is a skill. It can be learned. But it needs to be learned slowly, not over a couple of days or weeks.

It's a commonly quoted statistic that it takes three weeks, or twenty-one days, to create a new habit, and even longer for it to become a part of your personality. With my clients, I take that length of time and double it, just to ensure the new behaviors we create become part of who they are. It's a process; that's why I meet with my clients every other week. It takes time to let a new way of doing something sink in, and by meeting every two to three weeks (rather than, say, weekly), we're able to see much more progress from session to session. I never go to the next step with a client until I feel they have the skills to maintain and manage the area we recently completed, and that they're satisfied with their progress as well.

That's also why we spend a lot of time at our initial meeting developing and completing a needs assessment. There's no magic spell to make somebody organized. We establish which need is a top priority and work toward achieving that goal, then move forward from there. We create a plan of action. We figure out how to best tap their "inner organizer," and work to find the best organizational systems and products that suit them and their families. Sometimes we find the right solution on the first try. Sometimes it's trial and error.

> *Ability is one thing, but it is desire that drives a person away from a chaotic lifestyle.*

I'll say it again. You don't have to be born with a natural talent for organization. Sure, it helps, but it's not necessary. What I've found is that my clients who want to make changes in their lives, do, no matter what their "organizational aptitude" is. Ability is one thing, but it is desire that drives a person away from a chaotic lifestyle.

Here's an important thing to remember: Once you dig in, you're likely to discover that the skills you learn in one area will translate to other aspects of your life. For instance, when you learn how to sort your mail on a daily basis, you avoid that unsightly pile on your kitchen counter, and you set the stage for ongoing organization in other rooms of the house. Sharpening your daily decision-making skills allows you to let go of unused clothing and other household items by donating on a regular basis to your favorite charity. And it only gets better from there. You will be energized and motivated by embracing new organizational habits. You'll be amazed at your accomplishments, which will only serve to encourage you to tackle other areas of your home—and your life.

■ IT'S A LIFE-CHANGING STEP

As I tell my new clients, don't begin an organizational project unless you truly want to transform your life, not just your space.

Some people can spend thousands of dollars with a professional organizer and not learn the organizing skills they will need to maintain their space. I don't want the people I work with to become long-term clients. The last thing I want to do is encourage a dependent routine where the only way you can stay organized is by having a professional follow you around all day, giving advice and cleaning up messes. Give a man a fish, the saying goes, and you'll feed him for a day. But teach a man how to fish, and you'll feed him for a lifetime.

I feel the same way about teaching a person how to get organized. After reading this book, you're going to have the most organized fish on the block.

Chapter 4

How We're Wired

Some people get energized when their files are spread over their desk or across the floor like autumn leaves. A pile of client stuff here, a stack of bills there. I'm a little different. I like to take a neatly labeled file out of the cabinet, set it on my desk, open it, work on it, close it, put it back in the file, and then cross it off my to-do list. To some people, that sounds overly organized. And maybe it is. But that's the whole idea. Because my organizational system is designed to fit my personality type and play to my strengths, it works for me. For you, something completely different might make a lot more sense.

Because my organizational system is designed to fit my personality type and play to my strengths, it works for me.

It's a simple but integral matter of understanding

what makes a specific personality type tick. A primary goal with my clients is for them to say to themselves, "Aha! If I'm this kind of person, then maybe this type of organizational system would work for me."

If we get to that point, we're already halfway home.

Let's take a look at some of the elements that will help you create your own organizational process.

■ LEARNING STYLES

You can at least *see* the on-ramp to the organizational highway, so it's time to pack for the journey. When you pile the kids into the car for a road trip, you bring along some necessities: a map, luggage, snacks, and plenty of motion sickness medicine. It's the same thing when you embark on your journey to "Organizationville." The most important preparation for the trip is to identify your preferred method of learning. There are three recognized learning styles: auditory, visual, and kinesthetic.

■ AUDITORY

Auditory learners prefer to gather information through listening. They pay special attention to not only *what* is said, but *how* it is said, taking note of tone of voice, pitch, and other vocal inflections. Listening to a speaker or lecturer is preferred over written information. Another example would be listening to a book or study course on tape.

■ VISUAL

Visual learners get information by watching or reading. They often think in pictures or colors, and learn most effectively when they see something, such as labels, diagrams, or illustrations. Training videos are excellent tools for visual learners. It is estimated that as many as 85 percent of all adults respond well to visual learning.

■ KINESTHETIC

Kinesthetic learners like a hands-on, tactile approach to stimuli, learning by touching. While teaching our son to read, I discovered that, unlike his visual sister, he preferred writing his letters in the air, tracing them on my back or in a tray of sand. Years later when it came to studying spelling words, he practiced by using letter dice, handling the cubes while picking out the correct letters. I've always maintained that kinesthetic learners have all the fun!

Are you a visual learner? Do you prefer sorting your files by touch? Can you retain information just by listening to a lecturer, without taking notes? Knowing your learning style—and where to focus your organizational efforts—can make all the difference. Listen to your gut. Your initial thoughts about how you learn most effectively can play a big role in developing the skills it takes to kick chaos to the curb.

■ ■ ■ CASE STUDY: EMMA ■ ■ ■

One client, a teacher named Emma, was forced by her principal to hire me. Emma stacked things in piles, and they were threatening to touch the ceiling of her classroom. Craft projects sat unfinished in every corner of her room. She kept files and materials in her car. She lost her students' assignments. She missed appointments. The situation had unraveled to the point that if she hadn't sought some professional help to lessen her disorganization, she would have been fired. As you might imagine, her chaotic way of doing things was overtaking her life, filling her with dread about possibly being let go, and making her feel badly about her relationships with her students and their parents.

At our initial meeting, it became obvious that Emma was primarily a visual learner with a few kinesthetic tendencies. She really needed to *see* something before it sunk in. In her classroom, she simply couldn't find a filing system that worked for her, yet she felt she had to use a conventional file drawer that opened and closed. Everybody else used a traditional filing cabinet, she told herself. Why couldn't she? After talking with her about her learning style, we decided to try open-drawer filing. And you would be amazed at the difference it made.

She'd never considered open-drawer filing, which simply allows a person to keep files organized in a filing cabinet, only there's no top to the drawer. Nor had she considered color-coding her files: yellow for science, red for math, or blue for English. Embracing a color-coded system allowed Emma to see everything all the time, and made it simple to find a home for a file, report, or assignment as soon as it hit her desk. With her reliance on the visual, seeing her files, rather than hiding them away in a drawer, allowed her to make decisions about each piece of paper as it arrived. That simple change—to accommodate her learning style—made a tremendous impact on her career. Before we met, she was almost ready to quit teaching. Today, she's thriving. And so are her students.

Getting to know and embracing your learning style can quite literally change your life.

■ PERSONALITY STYLES

Just as important is your personality style. Are you creative? Artistic? Do you consider yourself an out-of-the-box thinker? Are you an extrovert or an introvert? Are you spontaneous, or do you enjoy schedules and rules? Are you left- or right-handed? Are you left- or right-brained?

All of these questions are important to help determine which organizational tools and systems might work best for you. But don't stop with the basics. Dig deep! What activities did you enjoy back in high school or college? What was your room like as a kid? What are your hobbies and interests now? Would you rather play a game of pickup basketball, or would you prefer playing in an organized league? Do you prefer to work on several projects all at once, or do

Getting to know and embracing your learning style can quite literally change your life.

you like to focus on one project until it's done, then move on to the next item?

> *Give yourself permission to recognize the individual you were created to be.*

Give yourself permission to recognize the individual you were created to be. Everybody's unique. The key is to identify and appreciate what makes you tick, then use that valuable information to find an organizational system that works for you.

■ WHICH TYPE ARE YOU?

There are hundreds—if not thousands—of personalities out there. Every stranger you pass on the street, every coworker in your office has different likes, dislikes, passions, preferences, and quirks.

Researchers Myers and Briggs identified sixteen distinct psychological types, and what they discovered makes a whole lot of sense. You may have taken their inventory already; if you haven't, I'd recommend it. (If you're interested in learning more about the Myers-Briggs Type Indicator, visit www.myersbriggs.org for more information.) The results can provide some solid insight into what makes us do what we do, how we interact with other people, and areas where we may need improvement.

What I call "organizational personality" is a little different. Yes, many of the characteristics are similar to standard psychological types, but I've found that a person's ability to organize is dependent on a wide variety of factors, from personality and environment to career and hobbies to friends and family.

To give you an idea of some of the most common characteristics I've encountered over the years, here are a few familiar organizational personality types. Since we're talking about the Road Called Chaos, I've associated each type with a vehicle. I've also included comments they might be heard saying about their travels.

Ladies and gentlemen, start your engines:

Model T. Model Ts are "old school," preferring to do things the way they've always done them. They're rooted in tradition and are generally averse to change. "The way I've done things has suited me fine for decades, thank you very much," they might say. "No need to change to a new-fangled way of living. Nothing works quite as well as the status quo."

Convertible. Convertibles, on the other hand, are adaptable, although sometimes to a fault. Creative and often zany, these are non-conformist, imaginative thinkers. If it rains, they put the top up. They quickly change to adapt to a situation, but can be perceived as waffling. "I used to put my current bills in a small desktop holder. While it worked great, I just saw an infomercial for a different product that promises to do the same thing. Maybe I should try that instead."

Bookmobile. Clean, orderly, and pristine, Bookmobiles are often perceived as overly systematic. Everything's in its place, neatly stacked, and intricately arranged. "Okay, who mixed the colored paper clips with the plain ones? Don't you realize we'll all live better lives if they stay COMPLETELY organized?"

Garbage trucks. The polar opposite of Bookmobiles, Garbage trucks are messes on wheels—stacking, piling, and tossing without regard for structure or order. They're easy going and sometimes oblivious to the chaos they're leaving in their wake. Many times they're accused of being slobs or packrats. "Don't call my home 'The Pit.' I know where everything is, even my water bills from 1968."

Race car. These zip from place to place, considering ideas at a breakneck pace. They discard some organizational ideas and programs on a moment's notice and quickly implement others, trying something new if the last thing doesn't work right away. They often trade practicality for speed—and the ability to multitask. "While I was returning emails last night, I was also watching an organizing cable show where I noticed a new product. I found it online and quickly ordered it!"

Station wagon. Station wagons are dependable and reliable, and don't vary from routine. They're not too flashy, but they usually do a nice job of getting from Point A to Point B. "This tote might be nearly twenty years old but it has always done a great job of holding my cleaning supplies. If it ain't broke, don't fix it."

Compact car. Compact cars dislike waste. They're economical, efficient, and tend to make decisions based upon the bottom line. "I can't throw away my appliance boxes; I got them free! Yes, I know I now have forty-seven of them in the garage, but you never know when you might need a sturdy container."

Luxury car. These people surround themselves with the very best products and services, no matter what the cost. If it's expensive, it's necessary—even if it's counterproductive or fosters disorganization. "That high-tech organizing gadget costs more? Then it must be effective. I'll take three."

Armored car. Security is what drives Armored cars. If there's risk involved, they'll opt for the safe bet every time. "I file EVERYTHING. Of course, once it goes in my filing cabinet, I'll probably never be able to find it, but at least I know it's there."

Motorcycle. These guys are riding solo, tied to nobody but themselves and listening to the call of the open road. "I think I should organize. Oh, wait. The weather is so gorgeous out. I'll go for a walk. Oh, wait…"

These are just the tip of the iceberg. Keep in mind there are very few people who fall neatly into just one of these categories. Maybe you recognized a few traits from several classifications. A little Luxury car, a little Motorcycle. That's perfectly normal. Our personalities are made up of the sum of our experiences, and it would surprise me if you saw yourself as strictly a Bookmobile or only a Model T. Instead, I'd encourage you to create your own classification. Ask yourself some hard questions about your habits, your likes and dislikes, your history, your experiences, and listen to what you're telling yourself. Don't put yourself in a box, which can sometimes manipulate a person into becoming what they *think* they should be, rather than what they *want* to become.

> *Ask yourself some hard questions… and listen to what you're telling yourself.*

Relying on other people's perceptions of what they *assume* you're like can actually cultivate your disorganization. Case in point: I recently worked with an accountant named Connie whose personality flew in the face of every stereotype I'd ever encountered. Humorless, hair in a bun, pencils lined up on her desk, right? Wrong.

■ ■ ■ CASE STUDY: CONNIE ■ ■ ■

Connie had spent a lifetime delaying decisions. Her office was a blizzard of documents from the past ten years, and none of them were in any specific order. Papers were haphazardly piled here and there, in boxes, in drawers, on the floor. She could no longer walk into her office, let alone use her desk. She began to migrate into the kitchen, and then, when that became full of paperwork, into the dining room.

She finally decided her office space had grown out of control, so she called me and we got right to work. Despite her background as a bean counter, we discovered she was a very visual and artistic person and, in fact, thought primarily in colors. If you don't mentally arrange things by color, it can be an odd concept to grasp, but to Connie it made all the sense in the world.

In her mind, all tax documents were blue, all personal documents were red, all bills were green, and all work-related files were yellow. Simple as that. So I suggested a filing tab product that could be color-coded and, just as important, was larger than a traditional filing tab, so we could include several lines of information on each label. Because of her visual learning style, the color-coded, large-print labels were exactly what she needed to be able to break through the clutter. All of a sudden, it clicked into place. She knew where things were located and could retrieve any document in a matter of seconds.

After we worked together for about six weeks, Connie told me her life had been transformed. Yes, her kitchen and office were looking great, but more importantly, she felt more confident, more secure, more responsible. Her adult children, who used to avoid her house because it was such a mess, were now coming to visit.

Good organization doesn't just transform spaces, it transforms lives.

■ DOUBLE TROUBLE

Good organization doesn't just transform spaces, it transforms lives.

When I speak to groups, someone inevitably asks one of these questions, "What do you do when you're the person who wants to get organized, but you're married to a pack rat?" or "What do you do if you're the 'happily sloppy' one, but you live with a neat freak? Our organizational styles are soooooo different."

It's a common concern. So what happens when two vastly different personality types are working against each other? To put it bluntly, it can be a challenge. Men may be from Mars and women may be from Venus, but opposite personality types may as well be from other solar systems. I'm very careful as I work with my clients to be respectful of others who share the same space.

This next case study is a perfect illustration of what can happen when a "Felix" marries an "Oscar." Sometimes, it's not pretty. The spouse who revels in order and structure might seem too rigid and uptight. The partner who prefers a more flexible lifestyle may seem disorganized, messy, or irresponsible. And they often feel judged by others.

But compromise is possible. If both people understand that their partner is approaching organization with the set of standards born from their personality type, it makes it a whole lot easier to deal with—and to reach an understanding.

Often, a wife hires me to help with "her" areas of the house. The husband sits in his recliner, rolling his eyes. I can tell he's thinking, "She'll never get organized. I've been trying to pressure her to get her act together for twenty years." But then something happens. The husband sees that his wife is not only learning organizing skills, but maintaining areas that have always been a problem. It takes time to earn his trust, but eventually I prove to him this isn't just smoke and mirrors. As a result, he becomes motivated and asks if he can work with me, too. People really can learn the skills it takes to get organized. And they can do it together, even if they come from completely different organizational universes.

■ CASE STUDY: ALLEN AND JESSICA ■

Jessica is an ultra-organized businesswoman. Allen is an artistic stay-at-home dad. If this was a sit-com, it'd be hilarious. But it's real life, folks, and the differences in their personality types—and the way those trickled over into their housekeeping styles—were beginning to cause friction.

Jessica and Allen asked me to get involved when they found they were beginning to argue about their lower-level family room. Honestly, it looked like a toy factory exploded. Puzzle pieces were strewn across the carpet, games were stacked on the coffee table, dolls poked their heads from every corner. A lack of proper storage was definitely an issue.

But even more important was how these two weren't connecting when it came to keeping (or, more accurately, *not* keeping) their house organized.

Because Allen was focused on the day-to-day operations of his young charges, he seemed oblivious to his surroundings. He would step through the toys on the way to the laundry room and not even bat an eyelash. Jessica, on the other hand, found it difficult to focus on anything but the mess.

The biggest thing they needed was a neutral third party to make suggestions on how they could come to an agreement over not only their specific issues in the basement, but how to maintain their home. They were both too close to the problem to see any solutions. Adding a professional organizer to the mix was just what they needed.

Their youngest child was a toddler, so I first suggested they turn the closet space under the stairs into a lockable storage area for art projects, games, and puzzles. Allen installed wire shelving, a light, and a lock, and now the children's items are kept safely out of the way. Mom and Dad no longer need to worry about the three-year-old wreaking havoc with glue or a hundred microscopic puzzle pieces. Best of all, visual, artistic Allen likes the openness of the shelves, and organized Jessica appreciates the labeled clear tubs of craft supplies and puzzles.

With immediate trouble averted, we turned our attention to some long-term compromises. Allen would work harder to keep the upstairs neat and tidy, and Jessica would lower her expectations about the basement. Over time, she began to accept that the family room was the kids' space, and it would never be magazine-cover perfect. My gentle reminders that they were in the season of life called "Parenthood" helped them relax a bit on the overall expectations of the family's space.

Each moved a little closer to the other's perspective. Neither was right. Neither was wrong. By acknowledging both of their distinct organizational styles—and compromising along the way—Allen and Jessica's life became smoother and far less stressful.

■ WHEN BAD HABITS ■ HAPPEN TO GOOD PEOPLE

What's your best quality? You could probably name several without much trouble. You're caring. You're loyal. You're kind. But what would life be like if your very best quality actually played a role in your disorganization? It happens. Sometimes, what ordinarily would be considered a positive aspect of someone's personality can snowball into a problem.

> *What ordinarily would be considered a positive aspect of someone's personality can snowball into a problem.*

■ ■ ■ CASE STUDY: ABIGAIL ■ ■ ■

Abigail spent most of her life buying gifts and cards for friends and relatives. When she'd see something in a store, she'd say, "Oh, my, Sally would love this." And then she'd buy the item, only to forget about it or misplace it when Sally's birthday finally came around. It didn't take long to realize that one of her personality traits was that she was extremely generous. Unfortunately, that aspect of her personality eventually backfired.

What started as an innocent habit of buying things for other people started to feed on itself. And by the time I came into the picture, she had accumulated over five hundred greeting cards. Very few of them were "Happy Birthday" cards; almost all were "Thinking of You" cards, bought for no specific purpose other than to tell someone she loved them.

Even more astonishing than the piles of cards was what seemed to be an unlimited number of ungiven gifts. They were everywhere: embroidered pillows in the attic, toy trains in the basement, baseball gloves sitting unused on the way up the stairs. She was almost literally pushed from her own house by a combination of her generous nature and a disorganized lifestyle.

After sorting through the many cards, we filed them into two drawers, using appropriate tabs to separate them into various categories. We also gathered more than one hundred gifts that had been scattered throughout her home. Abigail decided to rename a spare bedroom "The Gift Gallery," and, let me tell you, Macy's had nothing on this place. We displayed the many gifts she had purchased on open bookshelves and had a lot of fun creating a mini-boutique as we arranged items by subject: kids, female, animal-themed, elderly, and so on.

Abigail made a commitment to do her shopping at "The Gift Gallery," her new favorite boutique. If she couldn't find an appropriate gift on "her" store shelves, she would try to order something online, or send fresh flowers or a fruit basket—as long as it could be shipped directly to the recipient. The goal was to help her use the gifts she'd already purchased and avoid accumulating new clutter in the meantime.

By making the organizational process fun (and it was!), we increased the likelihood that Abigail would stick with her newly acquired skills.

■ INABILITY TO RECOGNIZE LIMITS

Work. Home. Family. In today's hustle-and-bustle society, overloading our plates with too many responsibilities, activities, and tasks is a much too common habit. And when you've got disorganized tendencies, it can be even tougher to keep it all together.

■ ■ ■ CASE STUDY: PATRICIA ■ ■ ■

Patricia is a "big picture" business person. She's very visual, spontaneous, and a creative thinker, so, like Mike the salesman, she was paying little attention to the efficiency of her office set-up. But Patricia had incorporated a whole other set of challenges into her work. In addition to working full-time from a home office, she was trying to keep an eye on two young children. That combination was a recipe for chaos—with a capital C.

For Patricia, trying to blend her business while taking care of her children left little time to do either well. She was multitasking so aggressively, hopping from task to task so indiscriminately, that things were beginning to fall through the cracks. She'd be talking to a customer on her cell phone, flipping through a filing cabinet, wiping her daughter's nose, and ordering groceries online—all at the same time. She was headed for a big crash. And she knew it.

We first tackled the functionality of the room. Her computer and client files were across the office from each other. Once we repositioned her equipment, she became much more efficient at her desk, since all of her client information was now right at her fingertips. Because she's so visual, I also recommended putting up a giant dry-erase board that could be seen no matter where she is in the room to help her keep track of all the projects she's working on. She could easily jot down a job's name, deadline, and status. She felt the dry-erase board took away her anxiety over her exploding business because she always knew what was currently happening. In essence, it removed a lot of mental clutter.

But the biggest challenge had to do with balancing her career with motherhood. As a mom myself, it broke my heart when one of Patricia's kids would come into her office, and the child would feel rebuffed or ignored because Mommy was on the phone. And because she was so inefficient during regular work hours, Patricia was finding that she was spending more and more time in the office at night and on weekends, further cutting into the kids' "Mom time." We talked about priorities, and decided that the biggest positive step she could take would be to invest in in-home childcare. That way, she could focus on work during the day, and the kids would get their mother's full—and much-deserved—attention after work hours.

> *Small steps toward an organized life can help you achieve your goals.*

I'm thrilled to report that it's paying off. Patricia is working far more efficiently by focusing solely on her job four days each week, and the kids are happy to have their mom back. Her decision to simplify and refocus her energy had a dramatic, lasting impact on her life and on her relationship with her kids.

Each of my clients has a different situation. Some are new parents, yearning for a tranquil moment. Others are working to dig themselves out of a lifetime of bad habits. But all of them are making progress. It's all about envisioning how you want to live your life and moving— however slowly—in that direction. Small steps toward an organized life can help you achieve your goals.

Chapter 5

Mapping Your Destination

Packrat. Neatnik. Slob. When you're organized—whatever that word means in regard to your particular learning and personality style—you're comfortable with your environment. You make it to appointments on time. You can find what you need, when you need it. You feel dependable and responsible. You feel calm.

It's a process to find what feels right. It doesn't matter whether you're naturally a "Felix" or an "Oscar," you can maximize your organizational aptitude based on what feels comfortable. Taking a good look at yourself, your learning style, and your personality type can start you down the right road.

To move forward down the path toward organization, it's important to map your destination. Now's not the time to roll up your sleeves and suddenly announce to your family or coworkers that you're no longer disorganized. Start out slowly. Determine exactly what you want to accomplish. Then outline the steps necessary to achieve your goals.

■ AUDREY'S GUIDELINES
■ TO GET YOU ON YOUR WAY

Here are 16 Rules to Remember when it comes to starting your journey:

1. **Surround yourself with support.** Many of you have friends and relatives who have made insensitive remarks such as, "Let me know when you're tired of living like this and I'll get a Dumpster for you." I think it's important to develop a support system during this important journey. But don't rely on people who have been pressuring you. It's easier to make tough decisions if you're coached by someone who isn't emotionally attached, like an impartial acquaintance or professional organizer. I like to refer to this person as an accountability partner. Note, I said "partner," someone who will help in a non-judgmental, non-threatening way, and who isn't afraid to ask the tough questions.

I often ask clients how long it has been since they've actually used an item they're considering hanging onto. If we get rid of it, can you borrow it from somebody else? Is it some information that's readily available on the Web? What is it costing you to store? If you're debating whether to keep something, do some quick math. Figure out how much you pay per square foot each month in rent or mortgage. Then determine how much you're paying to keep something you might not necessarily need. Do you really want to pay twenty bucks a month to store a box containing eight-track tapes, a chipped ceramic elephant, and an old college textbook?

If a trusted partner asks you those tough questions, eventually you'll be able to ask—and answer—them yourself. A client once told me she could hear my voice, even when I wasn't there. "It was as if you were sitting next to me and saying, 'You don't really need to save that piece of paper, do you?'" she said. Now that's what I like to hear. Being able to ask yourself the tough questions is an organizational skill that you can eventually possess.

If you want to locate a professional organizer in your area, a good resource is the National

> *I define "realistic" as practical and achievable.*

Association of Professional Organizers (www.napo.net). Believe it or not, there really is a professional organization of organized people! We even have an annual national convention. And yes, it's the most organized event you could ever imagine. After all, it's put on *by* organizers, *for* organizers.

2. **Set realistic goals.** I define "realistic" as practical and achievable. You can't do it all. Not all at once, anyway. So for some, setting realistic goals might mean redefining your expectations. Sometimes, it's just not possible to clean the house every week, and you might have to convince yourself that cleaning "just" twice a month is okay. If you have children, remind yourself that you're raising kids, not preparing for a *House Beautiful* photo shoot. In the same way, if you have a lot of organizing to do, choose a small area first, like a drawer, closet, dresser, or bookshelf instead of an entire room.

3. **Go the speed limit.** It's like any other big undertaking. You wouldn't start a diet simply by saying, "Okay, I'm going to lose a hundred pounds." Instead, we break it

down into identifiable, achievable goals. "I'll skip dessert today. I'll get to the gym four times this week. I'll cut calories until I've lost one pound." Nutritionists say the weight we take off slowly is more likely to stay off. Same with organizing. You didn't become disorganized overnight. It'll take some time to establish new habits and create new routines. Slow and steady progress helps ensure long-term success and guards against failures.

4. **Define the purpose of the space**. Whether it's a den, drawer, or desk, each area of your home or office has a purpose. By determining a space's reason for existing, it makes it harder to use it as a catch-all area. If a drawer is supposed to be for spatulas, then you'll need to find another place for your candles. If an item doesn't fit the defined purpose, then it doesn't stay in that area.

> *Slow and steady progress helps ensure long-term success and guards against failures.*

You may think having more space is the answer, but that's not always the case. In fact, a larger house can often mean more disorganization. An individual drowning in clutter called me after he and his wife had recently moved into their dream home. He said that in the past they had always been neat and organized and had never struggled with disorganization. I wasn't surprised to hear they had gone from 1,800 square feet to a whopping 4,000 square feet. With all that space, what could possibly be the problem, you ask? They had several extra bedrooms, closets, and cupboard space that had no defined purpose. And lots of square footage with no specific use is a dangerous combination. They just put items wherever they wanted and the rooms began to fill. In other words, delayed decisions.

There are exceptions, of course. Believe it or not, I'm a firm believer in junk drawers. I think it's a necessary part of staying organized. We've got to give ourselves permission to not be neat and tidy all the time. I tell clients that it's okay to delay occasional decisions—on a small scale—and have a small junk space that doesn't always have to be perfectly organized. When my children were young, I designated one of their dresser drawers as their "Treasure Drawer." As they've grown up, they've come to realize it's really their personal junk drawer. But when it won't close anymore, it's time to do some pitching. Because they've been given permission to have a little bit of clutter, they do a great job of keeping their mess confined to where it belongs. The problem comes when the whole house turns into one big junk space.

5. **Sort and purge.** Once you've defined the purpose of an area, it's time to sort and purge the items in that space. Your defined purpose will be the measuring stick you use to decide which items get to stay and which items need to go. I recommend that in order to stay focused on your task, you have three containers as you begin this process.

The first container should be a dark container for garbage. You know, the stuff you find at the back of a drawer or the piece to a game you no longer play—or no longer even have. When your work session is over, you'll take this garbage out to the garage, to the curb, anywhere out of the house. I say "dark" because if it was white or clear you might get a glimpse of some of these items throughout your work project and be tempted to "save" an item from the dump. Or worse yet, a family member will come by and see an item and remark, "You can't throw that away. I made that for you in the second grade!" (And he's the one heading off to college in the fall.)

The second container should be a large plastic sack. Lawn and leaf bags work great. This sack will be for non-garbage items you no longer need. These should be donated to your local charity, church, or others in need. Many charities send out postcards on a regular basis informing you when they'll be in your neighborhood. Some charities even send out their own large plastic bags that you can use as you collect items for donation. Call them—they'll be happy to come and pick them up. In the meantime, until they can collect your donations, put the bags in your garage, your car's trunk, or in a storage area of your home. You might be tempted to rummage through these items and second-guess a few of your decisions, so put them somewhere out of your everyday path.

I like to use a laundry basket for the third container. This is used for the items you want to keep—they just don't belong in the space you're working on. After your organizing session is over, you can carry your basket around and put away these items in other "homes."

6. **Create and assign a "home" for as many items as possible.** When you've been shopping and you bring something new home, do you know where it's going to go? If you can designate a specific place for an item, whether it's a closet shelf, drawer, cabinet, or filing drawer, it will not only get used more often, it will get put away, too. Determining an item's home can work wonders for getting kids to put stuff away. Once I designated a specific place for my children's arts and crafts, these items got played with more often and—*viola!*—they got put away, too.

7. **Don't rely on list-making.** Making lists can be a good way to kick off the organization process, but keep it within reason. I've found that some of my clients tend to go overboard with their newfound organizational skills and map out every second of every day. Sometimes, especially if they've never really been list makers, they quickly find they can't keep up with all the lists, which only adds to the clutter and feelings of failure. I recommend keeping it to just one daily and one weekly list. That helps prevent taking on too much, too fast, or failing at managing the many lists you've made.

8. **Respect others' spaces.** If you're organizing a part of the house other family members use, be sure to let them know of your intentions and desires for a more organized area. If they aren't present when the organizing takes place, show them where items now go and how any new systems work. If the space you want to organize belongs solely to another individual, they need to welcome the change and be present for the work. I recently got a call from a woman who was speaking softly, obviously trying to make sure her husband couldn't hear our conversation. She told me her hubby was going away on a three-day business trip, and she wanted me to come in and throw away his beloved magazine collection.

I knew right away from the panicked tone of her voice—and the fact that she eventually admitted she was calling me from inside a closet—that her husband wasn't exactly supportive of her thoughts on getting organized. Without his buy-in, or even reluctant acceptance, it would have been an uphill battle. When it comes to working with married people, I've learned to never enter hostile territory. Needless to say, I turned her down.

9. **Enforce a no-clutter zone.** Clearing piles of junk from the kitchen table might make it sparkle today, but without setting new boundaries and creating new habits, it could be back to "Messytown" tomorrow. Unless you set—and enforce—specific goals for keeping the table organized, your kids will still dump their homework on it, you'll still throw mail there, or your spouse will toss his or her keys on it. Clearing clutter is a good way to kick off a long-term change in habits, but once you achieve that clean slate, that's when the real work begins.

10. **Keep your chaos contained whenever possible.** When a person begins to make piles, they start out small: some stray mail here, some old magazines there. But then the piles get to be too overwhelming, too distracting, and the person moves to a clean part of the room, only to begin piling again. That's when the guilt and shame can really start to build. "Oh, boy," they think, "that pile keeps getting bigger. Oh, great, now I spilled coffee on it. Oops, I ruined that document. I'm such a loser." Eventually they avoid going into the room with all the clutter and start over again in a clean room. And pretty soon they have two rooms full of clutter, and they're looking for a third.

You can start making progress on a small scale. Even something as seemingly trivial as assigning a specific, nonnegotiable place to put your keys every day when you get home from work can work wonders for your emotional well-being.

11. **Don't let short-term solutions distract you from the big picture.** When company is coming over, many people have almost manic "sort-fests"—brief periods of moving piles, stashing trash, and filling boxes. The house seems clean for a few hours. But then, over time, the clutter returns, and things are actually worse than before.

Here's a prime example of how quickly and easily things can get out of hand when responding in a fit of panic. One day my client stashed a small pile of junk mail in her oven because someone was coming over. Then, human nature being what it is, she just let momentum take its course, and she kept throwing mail there because it was *easier than sorting through it*. After all, she rarely cooked, so she reasoned that the oven was a space just waiting to be utilized to its "fullest" potential. And besides, it was dark and no one ever looked in there. But every time she walked through her kitchen, she felt waves of nausea, guilt, and shame over-take her.

12. **Don't get too far off track.** Like a diet, it's okay to stray from your regimented rules and snack on an occasional piece of birthday cake. But when you find yourself reverting back to old habits, watch out. If paper was your weakness and you begin saying, "Oh, that pile of papers doesn't look so bad on the kitchen counter," then it's time to revisit the organizational principles that got you back into shape in the first place.

If I notice things are becoming a little too chaotic at work, I find it comforting to shut off my phone and Internet for a while so I'm not distracted by a constant barrage of calls and email. This allows me to refocus on whatever task is in front of me and not suc-cumb to the temptation of disorganization. And when I'm ready to plug back in, I'm refreshed, renewed, and—best of all—I can cross the task I just completed off my to-do list. We meticulous people love that!

13. **Stick with it.** Back to the diet analogy: When you lose weight, your waist starts to shrink. Your face thins out. You develop better eating habits. It's a transformation. Eventually, it becomes less about dieting,

and more about a lifestyle change. And if it's done right, the habits you adopt—and stick to—can stay with you for your entire life. Learning organizational skills is an investment in your future. And it can pay off in a big way.

14. **Don't overdo it.** On the other hand, keep in mind that extreme behavior can be counterproductive. I have people attend my presentations because they're already ultra-organized and they're looking for "just one more tip" on how to be even more organized. Some people's perceptions are a bit skewed. I had to let down a potential client who took me into her kitchen, threw open the pantry door, and said in an exasperated voice, "There. Can you believe how bad that looks?" It was as organized a cupboard as I'd ever seen. All the like-sized boxes were lined up in neat rows. All the labels on the cans were facing the same direction. I would love to have a pantry as pristine as that one. To her, though, it was a mess. If you find yourself with obsessive tendencies, you might need to talk to a professional. And I don't mean a professional organizer.

> *Learning organizational skills is an investment in your future.*

15. **Don't be tempted by shortcuts.** When I see organizing shows on TV giving easy answers, sometimes I cringe. It's not as simple as they make it seem. The people on those shows spent years, even decades, contributing to their chaotic environments. Having someone else come in and create order out of chaos—without teaching the homeowner the skills to manage it—is not doing anyone any favors. Will it help in the short-term? Sure. But if those cameras returned in a few weeks, they might be surprised at how quickly the house fell right back into chaos.

16. **Reward yourself.** I don't care whether you're four or forty: change is hard. As human beings, we are motivated by a variety of things. So as you begin to tackle your disorganization, be sure to build in a reward or two along the way. Perhaps you'll treat yourself to a massage or pedicure, lunch with a friend, or even a weekend getaway. Personally? My rewards are usually related to chocolate. The important thing is to treat yourself with something special.

Chapter 6

It's Not Always Easy

It's about now in the process when my clients ask themselves, "Why bother being organized? It can be such hard work." And they're right. Getting organized can be a difficult process, especially at the beginning, when you're flexing organizational muscles that haven't been used in a long time.

Fallout can occur. When an organizational breakthrough happens, it might not always be comfortable—at first. But, like anything worthwhile, working through the challenges of *getting* organized can only make you—and your ability to *stay* organized—stronger.

Throughout the process, there may be events that bring up unexpected emotions. When that happens, having an experienced professional organizer nearby may prove to be very valuable.

No, we're not counselors or psychologists, but we can help you understand why the seemingly simple task of cleaning out a desk drawer, for instance, can appear insurmountable.

You have to be ready to deal with the clutter, both externally and internally.

■ ■ ■ CASE STUDY: JOY ■ ■ ■

I met one woman who was an extreme packrat. Joy saved every tag from every Christmas present her family ever received. She'd even saved, and I'm not making this up, her babies' umbilical cords. In the first few minutes of our initial meeting, I asked her something: "Did you have a house fire when you were a child?" She stopped, as if she ran into a wall, then nodded her head yes.

Every cherished possession Joy had was taken from her as a child, so now she assigned an inordinate amount of value to everything, no matter how trivial or odd. Dealing with events from our childhood that shaped our organizational life is a big part of clearing the clutter. When Joy confronts the feelings behind the fire, she can move forward with purging the junk from her life.

■ ■ ■ CASE STUDY: SHEILA ■ ■ ■

Sheila hired me to help her organize her attic. Her parents died twenty-five years before, and she wanted my opinions on which of their possessions should be thrown away, and which should be donated or sold. She didn't have children to pass the belongings on to, and she felt it was time to get rid of the clutter.

When she took a look at the dusty beds, dressers, end tables, leather purses, and dolls—which she hadn't seen in fifteen years—she felt decades of emotions come surging back. "I can't deal with getting rid of this now," she told me, in tears. We made a pot of coffee and talked more about why the contents of her attic were affecting her so strongly, a quarter-century after her parents passed away.

Gently but firmly, I began to ask her some of the necessary tough questions. What would happen if she didn't make some decisions, and instead left the furniture in the attic? I finally phrased it this way, "If you were suddenly killed in a car accident, where would this stuff go?"

She shrugged, and we started talking about her family. She hadn't been particularly close to her siblings, or to her nieces and nephews, who were scattered across the country. I suggested that instead of selling the valuable antiques (and certainly as an alternative to throwing them away), she offer them to her relatives, many of whom were starting families of their own and would no doubt love antique furniture from their aunt.

For Sheila, the thought of passing along her family's possessions to a new generation of family members who would appreciate, use, and cherish them was enough. She was able to work through some of the feelings of loss the things in the attic brought up by visualizing that those possessions would find new homes—and have an impact on the lives of her loved ones.

What started as a struggle to get organized turned into an opportunity to build relationships with her relatives, many of whom she'd lost touch with. As I'd suspected, her nieces and nephews were thrilled to receive the furniture, both to use with their own families and as a link to their heritage.

Sheila's story is a great example of how important it is to deal with not only the outward manifestations of disorganization, but the internal issues that surround it as well.

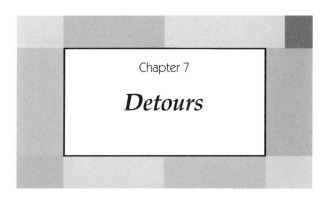

Chapter 7

Detours

No matter which personality type you are, no matter what your family of origin was like, you may have temporary setbacks on your journey to a more organized life. There will be challenges on the road to organization. Be ready, because you're bound to encounter them. But as long as you know they're out there, you can be prepared.

This is a good time to revisit some of the common reasons behind disorganization. These are often the same potholes that pop up along the road to getting and staying organized.

There will be challenges on the Road to Organization.

For most, it boils down to at least one of these hurdles you'll need to spend time working to overcome:

You get a flat tire. All of a sudden, your focus is turned to something else: a sick child, the death of a loved one, a lost job.

You run out of gas. You may begin having second thoughts about this journey when you consider what lies ahead. "I've got too much stuff. It's too exhausting. I don't think I'm capable."

You miss your exit. If you're not paying attention, you can get sidetracked. Or maybe you bought the wrong organizational product, and it's going to take renewed focus to find the right system or product for what you need.

You encounter roadblocks. Perhaps a spouse or other loved one decides they really don't want to change or, more importantly, they don't want *you* to change. This could be a major barrier in your path.

You're unsure of what direction to take. You get started down the right path, then suddenly come to a fork in the road and don't know where to go next. Instead of exploring the options before you, you face temptations to turn around and go back to living the way you used to.

There are plenty of other detours to navigate: chaotic home life, lack of knowledge about organizational tools, emotional attachment to "stuff." But the biggest challenge is an inability to make decisions. Often it's so much easier not to decide. And indecision can quickly turn even the smallest flake of chaos into a blizzard.

■ CLUTTER IS CAUSED
■ BY DELAYED DECISIONS

If you remember one thing from this book, remember this: People have clutter because of delayed decisions. Some people pay bills only when the stack on their desk gets too high and threatens to collapse. "I don't have to file until the inbox is full," others tell themselves. "I don't want to deal with it. I'm going to wait until later." Only "later" never comes, and the clutter continues to grow.

Sorting and purging can be exhausting, and many people postpone it as long as possible, which is understandable. But the ramifications of delaying getting organized can result in lost money, time, or emotional closure.

I met a woman who stuffed years worth of mail, including payroll checks and gift certificates, into a drawer instead of dealing with each item as it came in. "It's just easier," she said. But she changed her tune as soon as we started going through the drawer and she found she had stashed away literally thousands of dollars that could have come in awfully handy.

■ ■ ■ CASE STUDY: PETER ■ ■ ■

My client Peter had a carefree attitude with money. After all, he reasoned, he was single and really didn't have a lot of responsibilities. For many years, he stuffed large wads of cash into an oversized container, which he called his piggy bank. He didn't think it was important to keep an eye on every penny he earned. After some cajoling, he agreed to open it and dig in. Imagine his delight when he realized he had accumulated a lot of money—nearly eight thousand dollars! That's like finding a down payment on a house between the cushions of your couch.

■ ■ ■ CASE STUDY: AUDREY ■ ■ ■

Yes, I'm guilty of letting decisions pile up as well. Like many people, we had a spare bedroom where we'd stick stuff that didn't have a home.

Old client files, unused clothes, hobbies that had fallen by the wayside. I didn't really notice how bad it had gotten until a family friend came to live with us for a while, and we suddenly needed to clean out the bedroom. Reality came flying at us like a freight train. After seven years of delayed decisions, we discovered there was so much stuff in that room, we could barely see the bed. But our friend's arrival forced us to deal with the decisions we'd been putting off for years and years, and now the room is as organized as any place in our house.

It's easy to take a detour toward disorganization. But, with a well-planned route, it's just as easy to find your way back on track, particularly if you've brought the right tools along for the ride.

■ ■ ■ CASE STUDY: KRIS ■ ■ ■

My client Kris is an example of how someone with plenty of organizational skills can quickly become overwhelmed. Her whole life, the busy wife and mother of four boys relied heavily on regimen. She was an exercise fanatic. She printed out an electronic schedule and to-do list every day and followed it to the letter. She was extremely self-disciplined.

Then she started a home business in a spare bedroom and found that, despite her best efforts, the space quickly spun out of control. Kris was very controlled and organized in all aspects of her life—except this one room. The paper in her office was starting to develop a life of its own, creeping all over the floor, in stacks on her desk, sticking out of filing cabinets. What was going on?

It turns out that her natural inclination toward organization was actually working against her. She relied upon her regimen so much that, when something came into her life that didn't fit one of the specific categories she'd divided her life into, she didn't know what to do. She'd receive a schedule of community education classes, and because she didn't know exactly where to file it, it would end up on the floor. She had cooking newsletters, travel brochures, clothes catalogs—all things she might eventually develop an interest in. But because they didn't fit into the filing system she'd set up, the "hey-I-might-want-to-look-into-this-someday" materials didn't have a home, and ended up all over the place.

Kris is very goal-oriented, so I knew that if we talked about the importance of making decisions—or at least giving a piece of paper a home, however temporarily—she'd thrive. And she did! Based on her high-energy, fast-paced way of doing things, I suggested an open filing system to sit on her credenza right behind her desk, with dozens of categories, from Activities to Zinfandel, and everything in-between. Even though she still hates to file, she's developing the ability to put things where they belong. And if they don't belong in one of the categories we set up, she creates a new place for them.

Kris found herself getting off track, identified the detour, and worked to put herself back on the road.

And you can do the same thing.

Chapter 8

Keep on the Road

The challenges associated with getting organized can be overcome, especially if you're prepared. Take the time to understand what makes you *you*, and build an organizational program around your comfort level, not around what other people think you should do.

As you embark on your journey toward banishing chaos, keep in mind that repetition builds knowledge, skill, and confidence. The more you use your newfound organizational muscles, the easier it'll get. The longer you maintain your new way of doing things, the better your skills will develop. And, as you see the positive

> *Take the time to understand what makes you you, and build an organizational program around your comfort level, not around what other people think you should do.*

results you've achieved, the more your confidence will increase. Celebrate organizational triumphs, then push yourself a little harder to achieve your next goal.

By reading this book, you've taken an important first step. You've proven you're open to making a change. You're willing to learn more about why you're disorganized in the first place. You've realized there are numerous organizational options for your unique personality type. You're heading in the right direction.

You're already on your way. Stay on the course you've mapped out. Drive the speed limit.

And, for crying out loud, if you get lost, don't be afraid to ask for directions.

Resources

www.organizedaudrey.com—The online home of Organized Audrey, this site includes organizational tips for the home and office, links to Audrey's favorite organizing Web sites, and information about Audrey's consulting services, products, and workplace seminars.

www.napo.net—The National Association of Professional Organizers' site provides a great automated referral system designed to help you find a professional organizer in your area, as well as answers to frequently asked questions about working with an organizer.

www.nsgcd.org—The official site of the National Study Group on Chronic Disorganization features fact sheets, article reprints, and a referral service that offers help locating professional organizers who understand Chronic Disorganization issues.

Acknowledgements

When it comes to thanking people who played a role in this book project, my fear is I'm going to leave someone out. After all, that might be perceived as being disorganized!

My first thanks go to Maggie and Jake. Thank you for the meals you cooked, the errands you ran, and all those hugs you offered. You've been supportive and understanding. What a blessing you are to me.

Thank you, Mom and Dad, for your interest and kind words as this organizing business has grown.

To Bob and Pinky, the greatest in-laws anyone could ask for. It is impossible to place a value on the love and support you've shown.

To my collaborator, Brian Bellmont: You are a talented writer, and I am better for having worked with you. It's rumored that I'm a little quirky to work with at times. You handled me like a pro!

To my Cedar Valley Church family: Many of you have attended my public seminars and have watched this project come to life. Thank you for your caring support and prayers.

To my walking partner, Linda: What great memories! Even when I misread the clock at 4:00 A.M.

To Tonya: Thank you for your gentle reminders that I'm simply sharing God's ideas, not my own.

To the L.E.F.S.A. Ladies—Amy, Kim, and Lisa: Our friendship has allowed me to grow professionally and our discussions fostered this project. My desire is to encourage you as much as you have me.

To Rick & Marcy, Eric & Sherri, Pat & Mike: Thank you for reminding me of the faithfulness of God.

To Carol, Joey, and Kathleen: Your expertise and time spent reading the manuscript is so appreciated. It was helpful to have outsiders take a look at something that had become so familiar to me.

To Harry and Sharron at Expert Publishing: Your expertise has been invaluable in an area so foreign to me.

And finally, to my clients: Without you, there would be no book. I was privileged to work with each of you. You entrusted the most personal parts of your lives to me. I respect you for taking charge and changing your lives.

Organized Audrey

Audrey Thomas has helped thousands of people develop the organizational skills they need for a lifetime of peace and harmony at home and at work.

She began her organizational career in 1991; her company, Organized Audrey, LLC, exists to provide clients with quality information and skills that create a sense of serenity and order. Today, in addition to maintaining a full roster of home and business clients, she is an in-demand speaker, training employees of small companies, state agencies, and Fortune 500 corporations. Her entertaining seminars and workshops inspire others to understand disorganization—and take the first steps toward banishing chaos from their lives.

A frequent guest on radio and television programs, Audrey lives in Minnesota with her husband and two children.

She's seen it all: junk mail stuffed into kitchen appliances, piles of files ready to topple, computers overflowing with megabyte upon megabyte of electronic clutter.

As the founder of Organized Audrey LLC, Audrey Thomas has spent more than a decade in the trenches, teaching the skills that create efficiency, productivity, and life balance—in the home, home office, and workplace.

Her high-energy, participatory workshops are in demand for corporate Lunch & Learns, work/family programs, association meetings, leadership conferences, and CEU training sessions. She inspires audiences of executives, administrators, sales reps, educators, and employee groups to understand disorganization—and take the first steps toward banishing chaos from their lives.

Whether she's training employees of Fortune 500 corporations and medium size companies, schools and universities, or government agencies, Audrey customizes her seminars to your needs, weaving real-life stories from her years as a nationally known organizing expert into entertaining, dynamic, and memorable presentations.

For availability and booking information, call Audrey at (952) 944-2967 or contact her at
www.organizedaudrey.com

Organized Audrey Products

What's for Dinner? a home study course featuring the Menu Planning Workbook and DVD describing Organized Audrey's process for reducing the time, frustration, and expense associated with meal planning and preparation.

The workbook contains key support materials to help you plan your own menus, schedule meals, and develop custom grocery lists. There are exercises for you to complete as you progress through the course. Customers tell us they've saved thousands of dollars each year following Audrey's plan.

Broadening children's responsibilities adds to their self-esteem as well as confirming their importance in the family. As they become teenagers, they will appreciate their role in keeping the home running smoothly.

Skills & Responsibilities From Tots to Teens is a practical tool that will help you evaluate your progress in the parenting challenge and guide you in knowing what important skills your child needs to learn. In this booklet, age-appropriate lists and charts can be used to motivate and encourage youngsters in the training process.

Does the stress of holiday season preparations rob you of joy each year? If your head spins each year as you try to "keep it all together," you'll appreciate the **Hope for the Holidays** Organizer. This easy-to-use binder will keep and organize all your ideas, receipts, gift lists, and to-do lists all in one place.

Chapters include: Budgeting, Greeting Cards, Decorating, Entertaining, Gift Buying, Scheduling of Events, Stress Reducers, and many more.

Organized Audrey provides products and services that teach the knowledge and skills of organization, helping you transform your life, not just your space. To see these products and others:

Visit us on the Web at:

www.organizedaudrey.com

or call 952.944.2967